FRED VAN LENTE ★ RYA[N]

# ACTI[ON]
# PRESIDENTS

# #1

FRED VAN LENTE ★ RYAN DUNLAVEY

# ACTION PRESIDENTS

REAL HISTORY!
FAKE JOKES!

# GEORGE WASHINGTON!

HARPER alley

An Imprint of HarperCollinsPublishers

Harper Alley is an imprint of HarperCollins Publishers.

Action Presidents #1: George Washington!
For information address HarperCollins Children's Books, a division of HarperCollins Publishers,
195 Broadway, New York, NY 10007.
www.harpercollinschildrens.com

Library of Congress Control Number: 2017950229
ISBN 978-0-06-289118-1 (trade bdg.)
ISBN 978-0-06-289117-4 (pbk.)

The artist used Adobe Photoshop, a Wacom Cintiq tablet, and insomnia to create
the digital illustrations for this book.

20 21 22 23 24   GPS   10 9 8 7 6 5 4 3 2 1
❖
First Edition

For Dad, who taught me to love (and make fun of) history.
—FVL

In memory of Jim Dunlavey, my dad, who dragged me to
Mount Vernon too many times to count. It was worth it!
—Ryan

HEY, MAN!

STOP FILLING KIDS' HEADS WITH HOOEY!!

KICK!

GEORGE WASHINGTON

GAH!

Mason Locke "Parson" Weems (1759-1825), Well-Meaning Liar

WHO ARE YOU?!?

NOAH THE HISTORKEY!

"History" + "Turkey" (duh)

I WAS PARDONED BY THE WHITE HOUSE FOR THANKSGIVING, BUT ON ONE CONDITION:

NOAH, YOU MUST USE YOUR NEWFOUND FREEDOM TO SPREAD THE AWESOME AWESOMENESS OF HISTORY TO THE PEOPLE.

BUT IS THAT REALLY FREEDOM IF THERE ARE STRINGS ATTACHED?

SEEMS TO ME LIKE YOU JUST HAVE ME IN A CAGE BY ANOTHER NAME —

OR WE COULD ALWAYS GO WITH PLAN B...

OKAY! HISTORY! YOU GOT IT! NOAH'S YOUR BIRD!

2

PEOPLE *HERO-WORSHIPPED* THE USA'S FOUNDING FATHERS RIGHT AFTER THE REVOLUTION...

...SO OLD-TIMEY WRITERS LIKE PARSON, HERE, WANTED GEORGE TO SEEM *PERFECT* FROM BIRTH...

IS THAT THE TIME? GOTTA GO!

...AND THEY WANTED *YOU* TO WANT TO BE JUST LIKE *HIM*.

AND *YOU* DON'T?

*WHAT?* NO, I'M NOT YOUR PARENTS. I DON'T CARE WHAT YOU DO.

BUT I *DO* CARE ABOUT THE AWESOME *AWESOMENESS* OF HISTORY.

TOO OFTEN PEOPLE TALK ABOUT THE PAST LIKE IT'S A MOVIE YOU ALREADY KNOW THE ENDING TO – OR A FABLE THAT'S SUPPOSED TO HAVE SOME KIND OF A *MORAL* AT THE END.

YAY!

WASHINGTON

PEOPLE CAN TELL ALL THE TALL TALES THEY WANT –

– BUT *NOTHING* IS MORE AMAZING THAN THE *TRUTH!*

SO SIT BACK AND PREPARE TO BE BLOWN AWAY BY THE INCREDIBLE *TRUE* STORY OF...

3

ACTION PRESIDENT!

Okay, so for starters, George's dad, Augustine, didn't really grow cherries but *tobacco*.

He owned farms around the northern part of *Virginia*, the first and *oldest* British colony in North America.

WHAT'S THAT, SONNY? *SPEAK UP!*

#1

VA

Also, most of the *chopping* around there would have been done by enslaved African Americans.

Slaves harvested tobacco that was sold to agents from Britain called *"factors."*

Factors brought the tobacco back to Europe, and they in turn sold to Augustine goods *manufactured* in Europe that couldn't be easily found in North America.

For hundreds of years, this had been the relationship between Britain and her colonies: America could only sell its goods *to* the mother country, and could only *buy* goods from her too.

As long as *trade* kept flowing, the king pretty much *ignored* America, and let her govern herself.

For example, only the *colonies* would *raise taxes* directly on themselves.

I'M GONNA SAY THAT *LAST PART* BECOMES IMPORTANT *LATER*....

I BET! YOU WANT THE *STORY*, FOLLOW THE *MONEY*!

People didn't think of themselves as "Americans" back then but as people from Virginia or New Jersey. Most of all, they thought of themselves as *British!*

Like anyone who was *anybody* in the colonies, Augustine planned to send young George to school in London to learn to be a *proper British gentleman.*

But when George was just *eleven years old*, his father *died*, and his future became very *uncertain*.

He certainly would *not* be going to Britain for *school*.

NO!! NOT MY GEORGIE-PORGIE BABY! YOU HAVE TO STAY HERE AND HELP TAKE CARE OF YOUR LITTLE BROTHERS! YOU'RE THE MAN OF THE HOUSE NOW!!

He wanted to join the British Royal *Navy* like his older brother did but...

*NOOOO!* I CAN'T LET MY GEORGIE GET EATEN BY SHARKS OR MAROONED ON A DESERT ISLAND! I WON'T LET YOU!

>SIGH<

Finally, at *sixteen*, he had the opportunity to become a *surveyor* (someone who examines lands for maps or construction).

*NOOO!* NOT THE FRONTIER, GEORGIE-PORGIE-PUDDING-PIE! YOU'LL GET EATEN BY BEARS! YOU'LL GET SHOT AT BY INDIANS! YOU'LL –

LOOK, MOM, WE REALLY NEED THE MONEY.

BESIDES, I WANT ADVENTURE! I WANNA EXPLORE THE UNKNOWN!

AHH! HERE I AM! THE UNKNOWN!

MA! DON'T WAIT FOR ME FOR DINNER!

In those days, Virginia's "backyard" was what is now western Pennsylvania and Ohio: wilderness in which many tribes of Native Americans lived.

But the colony claimed ownership of it all, and surveyors like George had to go explore it so *maps* and *property lines* could be drawn.

In the frontier country, George learned to live in the wild, brave dangerous animals, and befriend Native Americans.

He had already earned quite a reputation by the time he was just twenty-one years old....

YOU'VE TRAVELED THE FRONTIER LIKE FEW *OTHERS*, YOUNG WASH-INGTON...

*Williamsburg*
Capital of Virginia (1699-1780)/
Colonial Theme Park (1932-now)

...SO THAT MAKES YOU THE *RIGHT LAD* FOR THIS *SECRET MISSION!*

AS YOU KNOW, NORTH OF *OUR* THIRTEEN COLONIES IS CANADA, PART OF *NEW FRANCE.*

Governor's Palace
(See "Places to Visit" in the back!)

WHAT YOU MAY *NOT* KNOW IS WHAT THOSE *SNEAKY PIERRES* HAVE BEEN UP TO *LATELY!*

RUMOR HAS IT THE FRENCH HAVE SNUCK DOWN FROM CANADA TO START BUILDING FORTS ON LAND *OUR* KING GAVE TO *MY* "OHIO COMPANY"!

*Robert Dinwiddie*
Virginia Lieutenant
Governor 1751-1758
(heavily into real estate)

WE CAN'T LET THEM *GET AWAY* WITH THIS, WASHINGTON. NO WE CAN'T! THE HONOR OF MY *BANK ACCOUNT* –

– ER –

– *VIRGINIA* IS AT STAKE!

YOUR MISSION, SHOULD YOU *CHOOSE* TO *ACCEPT* IT —

— WHICH YOU *WILL*, IF YOU KNOW WHAT'S GOOD FOR YOU —

— IS *TWO-FOLD!*

*ONE!* SURVEY THE BEST PLACE FOR WE BRITISH TO BUILD A FORT OUT THERE TO DEFEND MY — UH, *THE KING'S* LAND INTERESTS.

*TWO!* FIND WHOEVER'S IN CHARGE OF THOSE FRENCH JERKS AND TELL THEM TO HIGHTAIL IT BACK TO CANADA —

— IF *THEY* KNOW WHAT'S GOOD FOR *THEM!*

I'LL SEND *TWO* INTERPRETERS WITH YOU — *JAKE* KNOWS FRENCH; CHRIS KNOWS A BUNCH OF *INDIAN* LANGUAGES.

Jacob Van Braam
1729-1792
(Dutch Sword Master)

Christopher Gist
1706-1759
(Trapper & Translator)

SO WHAT DO YOU SAY, KID?

SAY YES.

WOW... THIS IS THE *ADVENTURE* I'VE BEEN DREAMING OF *ALL* MY LIFE....

AND BEST OF ALL, IT'S A *ROYAL* MISSION.... I'LL BE AN AGENT OF *KING GEORGE!*

MOM CAN'T *POSSIBLY* STOP ME!

I'LL *DO* IT, SIR!

GREAT! DON'T DIE, NOW!

13

The Half King led George and his friends to a spot just a few miles from the shore of Lake Erie.

I GUESS WE CAN SAY THIS FORT IS NO LONGER "RUMORED."

YUP.

FORT LE BOEUF (Totally really 100% real)

G-GREETINGS, YOUR EXCELLENCY. MY NAME IS GEORGE WASHINGTON.

I AM AN AGENT OF THE VIRGINIA COLONY.

Jacques Legardeur de Saint-Pierre
Knight of the Military Order of St. Louis (Fancy French Guy)

ARE YOU THE COMMANDER OF THIS FORT?

OUI.

THAT MEANS "YES"!

MAY I PRESENT YOU A MESSAGE FROM MY SOVEREIGN LORD, GEORGE II, KING OF ENGLAND?

OUI.

THAT ALSO MEANS "YES"!

HE'S READING THE MESSAGE!!

I CAN SEE THAT.

EXCELLENCY, PLEASE! VIRGINIA CAN'T LET YOU BUILD FORTS IN OUR TERRITORY, WHERE YOU CAN ATTACK US.

OMG, DID YOU SEE THAT? HE TOTALLY TORE THE MESSAGE UP!!

RIP SHRED

HE SAYS ...RE ...Y ICI ...LUI ...AIX. THEIR MISSION HERE IS ONE OF PEACE.

THEN WHAT ABOUT THE CANOES?

QUE ...TS? "WHAT CANOES?"

THOSE CANOES!

THERE MUST BE, LIKE, TWO HUNDRED OF THEM!

"BUT ...S JE I DON'T ...OIS SEE ANY ...DE CANOES." ...OTS.

THIS IS BAD!

THE ONLY REASON THEY'D NEED SO MANY CANOES IS TO TRANSPORT FIGHTERS DOWNRIVER TO VIRGINIA.

WE MUST WARN GOVERNOR DINWIDDIE AT ONCE!

16

17

18

19

George and Gist built a makeshift *raft* and barely made it down
the freezing river to Williamsburg.

George headed west again, this time with 159 men in his "Virginia Regiment."

BATTLE OF JUMONVILLE GLEN
May 28, 1754: Virginians + Ohio
Seneca vs. French Canadians

23

<MY POOR LITTLE BROTHER – MURDERED ON A MISSION OF PEACE!>*

* French

<WE WILL FIND THESE BRITISH BUTCHERS AND MAKE THEM PAY!!>**

** Louder French

Captain Louis Coulon de Villiers, Commander of Ft. Duquesne, Half Brother of Dead Guy

WHAT ARE YOU GUYS DOING?

GOVERNOR DINWIDDIE WANTS HIS FORT, AND THE FRENCH ARE COMING AFTER US ANYWAY, SO...

AND YOU'RE BUILDING IT...HERE?

UH...I'M GONNA TAKE MY WARRIORS AND, UH, STAND OVER THERE....

(THEY'RE ALL GOING TO DIE.)

I HEARD THAT!

24

# THE BATTLE of FORT NECESSITY

July 3, 1754:
French Canadians + Ottawas & Hurons vs. Virginians

YOU KILLED MY BROTHER! PREPARE TO DIE!!!

IT WAS AN ACCIDENT!

Fort Necessity
"That little thing in the meadow" – Half King

The Half King realized that George had built the fort within range of the surrounding heights – giving French and Native American sharpshooters perfect lines of fire into its center.

OW! QUIT IT!

PEW PEW PEW PEW

If muskets had been accurate at all in those days, none of the Virginians would have made it out of Fort Necessity alive.

PEW PEW PEW

Even still, George lost a third of his men by nightfall.

KRAKKK-A BOOOOM!

25

The fort was so badly made, bloody rainwater soon began to fill it....

WHEN I WAS DREAMING ABOUT *"ADVENTURE"* AS A KID, I DIDN'T THINK IT WOULD BE SO...

*...GROSS.*

GOOD NEWS, COLONEL!

THE FRENCH COMMANDER WILL LET US SURRENDER, AND THE SURVIVORS MAY GO HOME UNHARMED!

WHAT'S THE CATCH?

<THIS SAYS YOU *AGREE* WE ATTACKED YOU ONLY BECAUSE YOU KILLED OUR MESSENGERS!>

* French

I DON'T UNDERSTAND FRENCH — HE'S SAYING THIS MEANS "IT WAS AN ACCIDENT," RIGHT?

UH.... SURE?

*UGH...MY FIRST MILITARY ENGAGEMENT... AND I SURRENDER! THERE GOES THAT CAREER!*

SPOILER ALERT: It was also the *last* time George would ever surrender!

26

These two battles started what's known in the USA as

# THE FRENCH & INDIAN WAR

In which Britain and France, each with their own Native American allies, struggled for the sole right to colonize the continent.

27

George's fellow Americans, however, treated him like a *hero*.

One of their own had struck first against the enemy, held out against a much larger French force, and brought most of his men back home alive.

OUR HERO

Still, George had had enough of *adventure*. He resigned from Viginia's army and rented the home of his late older brother *Lawrence*, along with its tobacco fields and slaves.

*Mount Vernon* overlooked the Potomac River. From his house George could see the arrival of *warships* carrying British troops to fight the French.

HMM...I'M *STILL* THE BRITISH COLONIAL OFFICER WHO KNOWS THE MOST ABOUT THE AREA AROUND FORT DUQUESNE....

I BET THEY COULD USE MY HELP. MAYBE I'LL WRITE THEIR COMMANDER –

*NO!!*

George missed his first appointment with the British commander while arguing with his mother...

DON'T *GO*, GEORGIE-PORGIE! THOSE FRENCH MIGHT *CAPTURE* YOU AND MAKE YOU EAT ALL THAT *RICH FOOD* AND THOSE *HEAVY SAUCES!*

*MOOOOOM...* ENOUGH ALREADY.

...but he made the second one!

I CAN'T GIVE YOU A REAL *COMMISSION* IN THE BRITISH ARMY, GEORGE – BUT I CAN MAKE YOU MY INFORMAL AIDE!

AWWW, C'MON – JUST LEMME HAVE ONE!

Gen. Edward Braddock (1695-1755) Kind of Clueless

IN THE END, THE BRITISH EMPIRE WOULD *SUFFER* FOR NEVER ALLOWING GEORGE TO TAKE A "COMMISSION" – AN APPOINTMENT DIRECTLY FROM THE HEAD OF STATE (IN THIS CASE, THE KING OF ENGLAND).

IF THEY *HAD*, HISTORY, AGAIN, COULD HAVE BEEN QUITE *DIFFERENT!*

I ARREST YOU ALL IN THE NAME OF *GOOD KING GEORGE!*

IN CONGRESS July 4, 1776

ALTERNATE HISTORY

Instead, in May 1755, 23-year-old George headed west for a *third* adventure...even though he was very sick with dysentery (which makes you poop a lot).

UGGGH... MY BUTT HURTS SO BAD.

Saddle Pillow (for his butt)

29

# THE BATTLE of the MONONGAHELA

July 9, 1755:
French Canadians + Ottawas + Potawatomis
vs. British Regulars + Colonials

Braddock's men had walked right into a French/Indian force from Fort Duquesne rushing to ambush them.

GAHH!

NO PROBLEM, I'LL JUST GRAB ANOTHER HOR—

OR NOT.

THIS ISN'T GOING WELL.

Native American sharpshooters cut down the British officers until George (who, technically, was still just a civilian volunteer, after all) was the only one able to organize a retreat.

THIS WAY, MEN!!

GEORGE...RIDE BACK...FORTY MILES...TRY AND FIND...MORE MEN...KOF!

General Braddock would die of his wounds a week later.

George had to crawl at times to find the road in the dark forest...

>SNFF, SNFF< PHEW! HEY, STAND DOWNWIND IF YOU'RE GONNA DO THAT!

TOOT!

STOP FOOLING AROUND. WE GOTTA FIND THAT VIRGINIAN.

...and he was still suffering from dysentery.

When he found reinforcements, they were too scared to march.

EHHH... HARD TO BLAME THEM, AT THIS POINT....

33

British command unfairly blamed Braddock's defeat
on colonial cowardice and stupidity.

But, again, Virginia welcomed George as the hero who had organized the retreat! They made the young man commander in chief of all the colony's forces!

ER... YOU KNOW WE *LOST*, RIGHT?

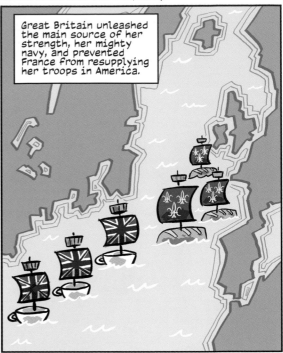

Great Britain unleashed the main source of her strength, her mighty navy, and prevented France from resupplying her troops in America.

George returned to Fort Duquesne with British and Virginian forces in 1758, only to discover the French set it on fire, then abandoned it once they learned they had no hope of resupply.

ALL THAT'S LEFT OF THE PLACE THAT WAS THE CAUSE OF ALL THIS FIGHTING AND DEATH IS A BRICK OUTLINE IN A PARK IN DOWNTOWN PITTSBURGH.

REALLY MAKES YOU THINK, HUH?

The War would go on for another five years and end in British victory, but the main fighting moved north. With *Virginia* safe, George resigned from the army and got married.

Because *Martha Dandridge Custis's* husband died without a will, she took control of his massive estate.

She was an excellent manager, and now had many of the same legal rights as men.

She was rich and powerful enough to marry whoever she wanted – or *not* marry again at all.

NOPE! NO! UH-UH!

But she met the tall, handsome war hero in March 1758 and it was love at first sight. They were married ten months later.

YES!

George's sister-in-law had died, leaving Mount Vernon to him, so he and Martha moved in with her two children, Patsy and Jack, from her previous marriage.

Sadly, neither child would live very long. Patsy died of complications due to epilepsy when she was just seventeen years old and Jack died of "camp fever" while serving in the American Revolution.

George took possession of one-third of the Custis estate – including the slaves.

But these remained Martha's "dower" slaves, given to her upon her first marriage. George could not sell (or free) them because they had to be passed down to his stepchildren and their heirs.

George's household, counting his slaves, was *huge*. At its height, *318* enslaved men, women, and children lived at Mount Vernon.

**10** slaves came from his father's will — George had been a slaveholder since he was *eleven* years old!

**15** came before his marriage.

**36** came when George inherited Mount Vernon.

**84** were his wife's "dower" slaves.

**40** he bought between his marriage and the Revolution.

Then there were the children of these various people, *born* into slavery because their parents were slaves.

Some say George was an especially *harsh* slave master; others say he was especially *kind*. What *is* known is that Mount Vernon's slaves were subjected to typical punishments like *beatings* and being sold away from their families for disobedience.

The slaves certainly did not *lack* for things to *do*. In addition to field hands, most of George's *overseers* were African Americans too, and many were carpenters, blacksmiths, and seamstresses. And a small army of servants worked at the main house.

George transformed Mount Vernon into a bustling mini-city of industry. With new land additions, it became *four* farms in *one*, but that did not stop him from rising before dawn every morning and tirelessly checking on every single one of his many projects.

ALL RIGHT, GEORGE, WE'RE READY TO TAKE IN THIS YEAR'S TOBACCO CROP....

I AM AFRAID YOU'RE GOING TO GO HOME EMPTY-HANDED THIS YEAR, GENTLEMEN — AND EVERY YEAR AFTER THAT!

British Factors
(remember them?)

I HAVE SWITCHED MY FIELDS WHOLLY OVER TO WHEAT AND CORN...

...CROPS I WILL SELL LOCALLY, IN VIRGINIA, FOR THEY CANNOT LAST THE VOYAGE TO BRITAIN.

BUT...HOW WILL YOU GET THE MANUFACTURED GOODS YOU NEED FROM ENGLAND?

GET THEM? MY PEOPLE ARE *MAKING* THEM RIGHT HERE IN *MOUNT VERNON!*

NOW SEE HERE, YOUNG MAN. YOUR *FATHER* DEALT WITH US FOR YEARS —

I AM SORRY, SIR, BUT I AM *NOT* MY FATHER.

VIRGINIA HAS ENOUGH BOUNTY HERSELF *HERE*...

...THAT I DO NOT NEED TO *WAIT* FOR WHAT'S ON THE OTHER SIDE OF THE OCEAN!

George was not the *only* colonial who felt this way.

For years, the presence of France in North America kept Britain and her colonies united against a common foe.

But Great Britain's victory in the war was decisive: She drove France out of the continent completely. Canada became British too!

Without a foreign enemy, there was nothing stopping the differences between the colonies and the motherland from boiling over into open hostility.

*EMPTY?!* UH-OH.

The new king, *George III,* took his throne in 1760, the year of France's defeat.

His empire was much bigger than his father's, but also *broker*: to win the war, Britain had borrowed more *money* than it ever had in her history.

The government decided to keep a large force of British soldiers in America in case France ever came back — and to make sure the colonists *behaved.*

WE'RE HERE TO PROTECT YOU!

UH... THANKS?

In London, capital of the Empire, the legislature, or *Parliament*, debated how to best *pay* for all these troops.

IT'S SIMPLE! LET'S MAKE THE *COLONISTS* PAY FOR THE SOLDIERS — AFTER ALL, IT'S FOR *THEIR* PROTECTION.

BUT...UH... WE'VE NEVER RAISED TAXES DIRECTLY *ON* THE COLONIES BEFORE? USUALLY *THEY* HANDLE THAT IN THEIR *OWN* ELECTED LEGISLATURES....

THE COLONIES DON'T HAVE A *VOTE* HERE IN PARLIAMENT, SO WE'VE NEVER TAKEN MONEY DIRECTLY FROM *THEM* TO RUN *OUR* GOVERNMENT.

AREN'T THEY... AREN'T THEY GOING TO BE *MAD*?

SO WHAT IF THEY *ARE*? THEY'RE THE KING'S SUBJECTS, AND THE KING *NEEDS* THIS MONEY TO DEFEND THEM!

I DON'T SEE WHAT THE PROBLEM IS HERE!

WELL... THERE *IS* THAT *GIANT SIGN*.

OH, I DON'T KNOW. I THINK WE CAN IGNORE THAT.

AFTER ALL, NEON SIGNS WON'T BE INVENTED FOR ANOTHER *150 YEARS*.

BAD IDEA

The colonial legislature in Virginia was called the *House of Burgesses.*

HEY! I SAID *BURGESSES,* WISE GUY.

IT'S AN OLD ENGLISH WORD THAT MEANS "TOWN OFFICIAL."

GEORGE HAD WON A SEAT THERE WHEN HE LEFT THE ARMY AND HAD BEEN A MEMBER EVER SINCE.

OOPS! SORRY.

THOUGH HE HAD "PATRIOT" LEANINGS, GEORGE WASN'T ONE OF THE *LEADERS* OF THE MOVEMENT.

NOT LIKE *THIS* GUY.

I SAY OUR COLONY'S CHARTER COMES FROM THE *KING,* NOT PARLIAMENT! *THEY* HAVE NO RIGHT TO TAX US LIKE THIS!

ONLY *LOCAL* GOVERNMENTS KNOW WHAT KIND OF TAXES THE PEOPLE CAN AND CAN'T BEAR! *WE* SHOULD BE THE ONES TO DO IT — AND *ONLY* US!

Patrick Henry (1736–1799) The "Liberty or Death" Guy

AND SINCE ALMOST NOBODY IS HERE TO *STOP* ME, I'M GOING TO SEND A NOTICE TO PARLIAMENT SAYING JUST *THAT!*

(Henry waited until all the pro-British burgesses left the room before calling for a vote on his notice.)

The relationship between Britain and her colonies just got worse and **worse** throughout the 1760s and early 1770s. Parliament would make taxes, America would protest, and Parliament would get rid of those taxes but then pass more.

George, like most patriots, did not want to break from Britain – *at first*. Patriots believed they were being abused by a bad Parliament. If they could get King George III to hear their arguments, they thought dumb laws could be struck down and dumb politicians could be stopped.

The colonists had no way of knowing that the harshest laws and punishments were in fact being directed *by* George III himself, who believed the protestors were nothing more than criminals and rebels.

**CRUSH THEM!!**

Violence in **Boston**, Massachusetts, was especially bad.

On the night of December 16, 1773, men dressed up like Native Americans, climbed aboard British ships in the harbor and threw the tea onboard into the water!

Parliament responded to the "Tea Party" by dissolving the charter of Massachusetts and blockading her port with the Royal Navy!

(WARNING: DID NOT HAPPEN LIKE THIS)

George attended a meeting of the House of Burgesses that voted for Virginia to observe a *Day of Prayer* for the people of Boston.

The Earl of Dunmore, Royal Governor of Virginia, quickly shut down the House!

YOU WON'T DO ANY MORE OF YOUR *REBEL PRAYING* IN HERE!

FINE! WE'LL START OUR *OWN* HOUSE! NYAHH!

The thirteen colonies sent delegates to a Continental Congress in centrally located *Philadelphia*, Pennsylvania, for a joint response to Great Britain. George was elected as one of the Virginia representatives.

He arrived with his personal valet, *William Lee*, whom he had bought as a teenager from a neighboring plantation in 1768.

William rose every morning with George and didn't go to bed until after he did.

It was said that Will was the *second-best rider* in all of Virginia –

– second only to *George*, whom he had to keep *up* with.

You could call them *friends*, if you could be friends with someone who could legally beat, kill, or banish you, at any moment, for any reason.

DO I *HAVE* TO WEAR THE *TURBAN*?

I THINK YOU LOOK *GREAT*!

YOU DON'T HAVE TO *WEAR* IT!

As a famous war hero with an exotically dressed slave, George made quite an impression on the other delegates. He was the only Congressman to show up in *full military uniform.*

Even people who knew George by reputation didn't expect how *tall* he was.

At *six foot two*, he towered over most people in colonial days, who were shorter than us.

From all his exercise at Mount Vernon, he had also gained incredible *strength.*

WHEN YOU BEAT MY PITCH, YOUNG GENTLEMEN, I'LL TRY AGAIN.

"IRON BAR"
(i.e. Colonial Video Game)

He *rarely* spoke, and when he did, he said something *important.*

Everyone was impressed – he still followed the "Rules of Civility & Decent Behavior" he had learned as a kid!

There was *another* explanation for his closed-mouthedness, though.

*HOPE NOBODY CALLS ON ME....MY TEETH REALLY HURT TODAY!*

George's *teeth* were a lifelong source of pain and misery to him.

He had his first tooth pulled in 1756 and kept getting them pulled until he was a very old man.

He told fellow Continental Congressman *John Adams* his teeth had gone bad from him cracking too many *walnuts* with them when he was a kid.

*HEY, JOHN!*

*WHAT?*

John Adams (1735-1826) Chief Massachusetts Delegate

*CHECK IT OUT!*

KSSSHHH!

*GAHHH!*

Dentists weren't very common back then, and a lot of people had barbers, and even blacksmiths, pull bad teeth.

HOLD *STILL*....

It hurt so much to eat, he preferred soft foods, like *pickled tripe,* aka cow intestines....

SLORP GORP GUZZLE SLOP

(an acquired taste)

HE HAD *WOODEN* TEETH, RIGHT?

NO, GEORGE WAS *RICH.* HE COULD AFFORD *BETTER* THAN WOOD.

HIS FALSE TEETH WERE MADE OF...WELL, *TEETH:* OTHER PEOPLE'S AND HIS OWN PULLED ONES, REATTACHED WITH METAL AND WIRE...

...ALONG WITH SOME *HIPPO* IVORY.

They hurt George almost as much as his real teeth, distorting his face and making his upper lip jut out.

You can see that pretty clearly even on his portrait on the one-dollar bill.

49

GENTLEMEN OF THE CONGRESS! AS YOU KNOW, WHEN BRITISH TROOPS TRIED TO SEIZE THE COLONY'S ARMS AND GUNPOWDER AT *LEXINGTON AND CONCORD*, OUR MASSACHUSETTS MILITIA BEAT THEM BACK —

— ALL THE WAY TO BOSTON! AND TODAY I HAVE RECEIVED *NEWS* FROM THAT CITY:

John Adams

HIS MAJESTY'S ARMY LAUNCHED A MAJOR ATTACK TO TAKE BACK MILITIA POSITIONS ON THE HILLS AROUND THE HARBOR —

(— THE FIGHT WAS OVER BREED'S HILL, NOT *BUNKER HILL*, AS YOU MAY HAVE HEARD —)

— AGAIN, THE BRITISH WERE BEAT BACK, BUT NOT WITHOUT *HUGE* CASUALTIES ON BOTH SIDES!

IT MUST NOW BE CLEAR THERE IS TO BE *WAR* BETWEEN US! SO WE MUST RAISE AN ARMY TO HELP MASSACHUSETTS — A *CONTINENTAL* ARMY —

— AND I SAY THE ONLY MAN TO LEAD IT IS THE DELEGATE FROM VIRGINIA, *COLONEL GEORGE WASHINGTON!*

HEAR! HEAR!

I THINK AS LONG AS HE DOESN'T HAVE TO *OPEN HIS MOUTH*, HE'LL DO IT!

YAAAAAYY!!

Really, George wanted only to command the armies of *Virginia*, but he felt like he couldn't refuse, under the circumstances.

With the rebels holding the hills surrounding Boston Harbor, the British couldn't defend their position. When George and Will arrived for him to take command of the army, the enemy left the city.

I'VE TAKEN BOSTON WITHOUT FIRING A SHOT!

GREATEST! COMMANDER IN CHIEF! **EVER!**

But deep down, George knew the fight was just *beginning*.

COLONEL! TELL YOUR MEN TO STOP *WHIZZING* IN THEIR OWN FORTIFICATIONS! IT'S GROSS!

I COULDN'T DO THAT, SIR. ALL US OFFICERS OF THE PENNSYLVANIA RIFLEMEN ARE *ELECTED* BY THE MEN!

AND IF I START GIVING THEM ORDERS, THEY MIGHT NOT *LIKE* ME ANYMORE!

BUT AS AN OFFICER, IT IS YOUR *JOB* TO GIVE ORDERS!

SHHH! DON'T SAY THAT SO *LOUD!*

I COULD LOSE THE NEXT ELECTION!

This was his first experience leading a "free" army. And George didn't like it.

The Continental Army was made up of militiamen from *thirteen* separate colonies, each with their own special way of doing things.

WHOA *WHOA* WHOA!!

HOW'D *YOU* GET A GUN?!

YOU! WHO ARE YOU?

COLONEL JOHN GLOVER, EXCELLENCY, OF THE 14TH MASSACHUSETTS.

THESE ARE YOUR MEN?

SURE. THEY'RE MY NEIGHBORS IN MARBLEHEAD. SOME OF THEM ARE SAILORS ON MY MERCHANT SHIPS.

WE WANT TO FIGHT FOR OUR COUNTRY AS FREE MEN OF COLOR. WHAT'S THE BIG DEAL?

FOR ONE THING, YOU'RE MAKING A LOT OF THE OTHER WHITE GUYS *UNCOMFORT-ABLE.*

WHERE I COME FROM, WE'RE USED TO ONLY SEEING *BLACK PEOPLE* AS *SLAVES.*

SO? THAT'S *YOUR* PROBLEM.

ALL RIGHT, LOOK. YOU GUYS WHO ALREADY JOINED UP, YOU CAN STAY.

BUT NO *NEW* FREE BLACKS, OKAY? YOU'RE GONNA UPSET THE RACISTS.

WHO CARES WHAT *THEY* THINK?

HEY! *I'D* RATHER HAVE A *RIFLE* THAN A *TURBAN!*

WE'LL TALK ABOUT IT LATER.

Few of his men had been outside their home colonies, let alone met people from the *other colonies.*

These colonial militias had been raised to defend against attacks by Native Americans and put down slave rebellions. They weren't used to European-style military *discipline,* much less fighting alongside black soldiers.

One day, white Virginia riflemen and Glover's multiracial regiment got into a nasty fight.

**One thousand** men were involved — more than fought at Lexington and Concord!

STOP! *STOP!*

An eyewitness reported seeing George and William Lee riding into the center of the riot....

GRAB!

HOW CAN WE HOPE TO BEAT THE **BRITISH...**

...IF WE KILL EACH OTHER FIRST?!

And so "hostile feelings between two of its best regiments" were "extinguished by **one man.**"

54

The next obvious place for a British attack was *New York City,* right smack-dab in the middle of the colonies.

George relocated most of his troops there and began building forts around Manhattan and Brooklyn.

WHAT DID YOU GET FROM CONGRESS?

HMMM... ADAMS AND THEM HAVE DECIDED THAT REJOINING THE BRITISH EMPIRE IS NO LONGER AN OPTION.

THE MEN ARE TO BE GATHERED AND AT THE HEAD OF EACH BRIGADE SHOULD BE READ THIS... *DECLARATION.*

WE HOLD THESE TRUTHS TO BE SELF-EVIDENT, THAT ALL MEN ARE CREATED EQUAL....

HUZZAH! HUZZAH! HUZZAH!

In CONGRESS July 4, 1776
A DECLARATION
UNITED STATES OF AMER

July 9, 1776

THERE'S NO GOING BACK NOW, BOYS!

WE'RE TO BE *INDEPENDENT* OF KING GEORGIE FOREVER!

*HEY!* THERE'S THAT STATUE OF OLE GEORGE III ON THE *BOWLING GREEN!*

55

TEAR IT DOWN! TEAR IT DOWN!

WAIT — WHAT? NO, DON'T *DO* THAT!

STOP! THAT'S NOT YOURS — LEAVE IT BE!

KLANG

HOOORRR AAAAAYYY!

ALL THIS DISOBEDIENT... ROWDINESS! I'M SO EMBARRASSED!

THE STATUE'S MADE OF *LEAD*, SO I HEAR THEY'RE GOING TO MELT IT DOWN INTO *MUSKET BALLS....*

(The ladies of Litchfield, Connecticut, did this.)

By this time, the British had assigned new commanders to run the war in America, the **Brothers Howe:** William was an army general, and Richard was a navy admiral.

WAR BROS!

The Howes landed a massive force on Staten Island and prepared for the largest *sea-to-land assault* in world history, matched only by *D-Day* 168 years later!

One soldier from Maryland wrote, "I thought all **London** was afloat!"

WE'RE, UH, GONNA NEED A BIGGER ARMY.

George hoped to draw the British into attacking a heavily guarded position like Bunker (uh, *Breed's*) Hill, but it became more and more obvious the city was too big, and too spread out across too many islands, to defend against such a large force.

Admiral Howe sailed his ship up and down the Hudson River, mocking the American positions.

THE SUSPENSE IS KILLING ME! WHAT ARE THEY WAITING FOR?

On August 15 George found out, when two convoys arrived on Staten Island full of...

# HESSIANS

These were mercenaries, or soldiers-for-hire, from the German state of Hesse-Cassel.

G.I. GERMAN

BREAK IN CASE OF WAR

America was a *big* country, and the king of England thought (correctly) he'd need a lot of men to hold it. He started negotiating with the Hessian Count in 1774, long before the war actually *started*.

Hesse was fairly *poor* and her rulers made a lot of money selling fighters to foreigners like King George III.

LEMME GET... UH... *THIRTY THOUSAND*?

Landgraf (Count) Friedrich Wilhelm II, Soldier Salesman

Hessians were *tough.* War-for-hire was a way of life for them. Boys had to register for military service beginning at age *seven* every Easter.

HUT! HUT! HUT!

* "rebels"

CURSE THESE *REBELLER** WITH THEIR NONSENSE TALK OF "LIBERTY"...

...WHICH JUST GIVES THE *GREEDY* FREEDOM TO *STEAL!*

TOGETHER WE RUN THEM OFF LIKE THE COWARDS THEY ARE, *JA?*

George thought the British would attack Manhattan first, and so kept most of his troops there...but he was *wrong*.

The British landed on *Brooklyn* instead and began looking for weaknesses in the American lines. They found some on northern Long Island.

They circled around the American lines and cut their way through the forest with saws and axes, completely surprising the colonials when they burst from the woods.

The troops simply *ran* – headlong into George! He tried to stop them with his horse whip, but they just kept running!

Troops from Delaware and Maryland heroically stood against the oncoming onslaught of British troops long enough for the Americans to fall back.

Part of the Empire's strategy was to terrorize the Americans and crush their will to resist.

Hessians were ordered to take no prisoners, and speared the rebels to the trees with bayonets, the knives mounted to their rifles.

Discovering that many of the American officers were tailors or mechanics or barbers – not men of higher social standing, as they were – the Europeans would beat them mercilessly or harness them to cannons.

HA-HA! PEASANTS!

George and the nearly ten thousand American troops left rushed to the East River. Admiral Howe was ready to cut him off and trap them.

But! A massive rainfall, followed by a heavy fog, allowed George to organize the men and retreat in boats to Manhattan.

WHICH WAY DID THEY GO? WHICH WAY DID THEY GO?

The Howes pursued George into New York City proper and all the way up Manhattan Island.

The attacks – and the *humiliations* – did not let up.

At a battle near what's now 33rd Street, Americans again ran away. Furious, George cried out:

"GOOD GOD! HAVE I GOT SUCH TROOPS AS THESE?"

In Harlem, a British bugler showed his contempt for the fleeing Americans:

IS THAT... A *FOX CHASE* BUGLE HORN?

*ATTACK!*

Finally, George and his men had to escape across the Hudson River, into New Jersey.

He watched through a glass as the last fort on Manhattan Island, Fort *Washington*, fell. Many who tried to surrender were killed while they begged for mercy.

George did not *cry out* this time but instead simply *cried*.

It was the lowest point in his long career. All seemed lost.

But he summoned the inner strength to not give up.
And that meant retreating. More and more retreating....

WHERE... ARE WE? NEW JERSEY?

NO... PENNSYLVANIA!

Their summer clothes had been turned to rags.

One Pennsylvanian observed, "If the War is continued into the winter, the British troops will be scared at the sight of our men, for as they had never fought with naked men."

Meanwhile, the king had **knighted** General Howe for his spectacular victory in New York City.

Believing the Continental Army to be essentially defeated, **Sir** William placed Hessians up and down the Delaware River to guard against the Americans...

...while he sent the bulk of his army across New Jersey to keep the peace among a rowdy populace that was fighting back against widespread looting by the occupying army.

(To be fair, the American army did plenty of looting itself. Though both sides banned stealing from civilians, supplies were hard to come by and soldiers were hungry.)

This was *the* problem the British would have over and over during the war: America is really, really, really *big*.

Even with their Hessians, at no point did King George III have enough men to cover the whole *country,* or even a single colony!

...NGGK... CAN'T... QUITE... REACH!

A Hessian force was assigned to guard Trenton, New Jersey, which by that point had been mostly abandoned.

The Hessian engineers told their commander, Colonel Johann Rall, that he should build defenses around the town. He replied...

*"Poop upon Poop!" (rough translation)

"SCHEISZER BEY SCHEISZ!* LET THEM COME.... WE WILL GO AT THEM WITH THE BAYONET."

Another Hessian later wrote, "It never struck [Rall] that the rebels might attack *us*, and therefore he made no preparations against an attack."

And why should he? He had *crushed* the Americans every time they fought.

The lack of Hessian defenses, however, did not go *unnoticed....*

HMMMM...

YOU MAY HAVE HEARD THAT THE HESSIANS WERE *DRUNK* FROM CELEBRATING CHRISTMAS WHEN GEORGE ATTACKED THEM — THEY *WEREN'T.*

LET ME GUESS...THE *TRUTH* IS EVEN CRAZIER!

YOU KNOW IT!

A *British spy* knew of the meeting in which George and his officers had decided to attack Rall right after Christmas.

WE MUST ACT *NOW* AND TRY FOR A VICTORY, *ANY* VICTORY, OR THE WHOLE *REVOLUTION* MAY BE LOST!

So Rall was warned *ahead of time* he would be attacked! His response?

LET THEM COME.

RALL, JOHANN

o·ver·con·fi·dent (ō'vər-kän-fə-dənt) adj. excessively confident; presumptuous.

A massive snowstorm rolled in, so Rall *canceled* the morning's patrol.

COME BACK IN! NO ONE WOULD *DARE* ATTACK US IN *THIS* MESS!

64

Washington's troops crossed the Delaware River in flat longboats, everyone having to **stand** to get as many people as possible on board.

There was a **waterfall** near Trenton and the massive chunks of ice in the frigid river were moving downstream **fast**, threatening to overturn the boats.

Three groups of American troops **tried** but only one – George's – actually made it across the treacherous waters to New Jersey.

Miraculously, not a man, a horse, or a cannon was lost.

On the march to Trenton, George placed guards along the road and ordered them to not let anyone pass unless they knew the secret password:

Victory or Death

The march was almost as treacherous as the river crossing, and as plagued by wind and ice.

Two soldiers who had survived the Delaware stopped to rest by the side of the road but **fell asleep** and **froze to death.**

At one point, George's horse began to slip, and soldiers were stunned to see him lift the animal back to its feet by its own mane!

**HOW** DID YOU **DO** THAT?!?

They reached Trenton just after sunrise, about four hours behind schedule.

WHERE DID YOU COME FROM? WHAT ARE YOU DOING HERE?

4th Virginia Regiment (Continental Army)

A HESSIAN SHOT AND KILLED ONE OF OUR MEN FROM THIS SIDE OF THE RIVER, AND WE'RE TO TAKE REVENGE!

SO WE **ATTACKED TRENTON!**

YOU... YOU DID **WHAT?!**

YEAH, WE SCARED THE HECK OUT OF THEM!

COLONEL RALL EVEN SENT OUT RIDERS TO CATCH US, BUT THE STORM DROVE 'EM BACK!

HOO BOY, YOU SHOULDA SEEN THE LOOKS ON THEIR FACES!

George's men said they'd never seen him this *mad* before.

"YOU, SIR! YOU, SIR, MAY HAVE **RUINED** ALL MY PLANS BY HAVING PUT THEM ON THEIR **GUARD!**"

They had no choice but to **move quickly.**

# THE BATTLE of TRENTON

December 26, 1776:
Continentals vs Hessians

George led the central attack against Trenton himself, through a thick flurry of snow in a long trot across an open field.

Hessian sentries could barely make out the shapes of men coming from behind the white curtain of the storm.

DER FEIND! HERAUS! HERAUS!

"The Enemy! Turn out! Turn out!"

The Hessians were alerted by gunfire and responded quickly, but they were heavily outnumbered.

WHAT'S THE MATTER?

DO YOU NOT HEAR THE FIRING?

I WILL BE THERE IMMEDIATELY!

The attack and the weather confused the enemy. Rall was told that Americans had surrounded the town. They hadn't – if Rall had sent for help, George might have been surrounded himself.

WUH BOOOM!

But Rall chose to counterattack *inside* the town, leaving the Hessians open to fire from American cannons.

I ALWAYS AIM FOR THE *OFFICERS...*

...I LEARNED THAT FROM THE INDIANS!

SOUNDS LIKE THEY HAD THE RIGHT IDEA!

As Colonel Rall turned to comfort a fallen officer, he himself was shot twice in the side. He was carried to a church and laid on a pew. He died later that night.

*KRAK!*

*UGH!*

Colonel Rall's men loved him and his loss sapped their will to fight.

SWITCH FROM ROUND SHOT TO CANISTER!

SIR YES SIR!

*Round shot* = Regular cannonball
*Canister* = Literally, a can filled with a whole bunch of little cannonballs

SIR – THEY HAVE STRUCK!

STRUCK!

YES, THEIR COLORS ARE DOWN.

SO THEY ARE.

All the Hessians surrendered. The Americans
didn't lose a single man in the fight.

It was the first real victory of George's career, and while Trenton itself wasn't all *that* important from a military point of view...

...the *dramatic* quality of the win, after so many defeats, breathed new life into the Revolution.

The average American began to associate George *with* the Revolution itself!

As early as 1779 Americans began to celebrate his *birthday* along with the Fourth of July, calling him the "Father of his Country"!

BUT — THERE ISN'T ACTUALLY A *COUNTRY* YET!

DETAILS, DETAILS...

HE CERTAINLY ACTED LIKE HE WAS SERVING A CAUSE *HIGHER* THAN HIMSELF.

GEORGE MADE CAPTURED LOYALISTS AFTER TRENTON SWEAR AN OATH NOT TO THE COLONY OF NEW JERSEY OR THE CONTINENTAL CONGRESS —

— BUT "THE UNITED STATES," THE NAME FOR THE ALLIANCE OF COLONIES. THIS ANNOYED A LOT OF PATRIOTS (PARTICULARLY THE BIGWIGS IN NEW JERSEY)!

In those days, wars typically took *winter breaks* because the weather made it too hard to fight (that's partly why George's attack on Trenton was so unusual).

In December 1777, the Continental Army arrived at *Valley Forge*, Pennsylvania, to make their winter camp.

Valley Forge was just twenty miles from *Philadelphia*, which the Brothers Howe had taken with barely a shot.

The Americans starved in their camp because the British could pay for food with good *pounds sterling* (silver)...

...while George had mostly *worthless* paper money printed by the Continental Congress.

YOU ONLY BROUGHT $15,678 USA BUCKS? SORRY, YOU'RE ABOUT $230,671 SHORT.

OKAY.

JUST GIVE ME THAT JUICY FRUIT, THEN.

*MONEY* WAS A MAJOR PROBLEM, IF NOT *THE* MAJOR PROBLEM, FOR THE CONTINENTAL ARMY.

THE FIRST CONSTITUTION OF THE INFANT UNITED STATES HAD BEEN DRAWN UP BY THE CONTINENTAL CONGRESS IN THE FORM OF *ARTICLES OF CONFEDERATION*.

Under the articles, the US was a loose conglomerate of thirteen mini-countries. The Congress had no power to *tax* and thus *make* those states help pay for the war effort.

But hardship can **strengthen** the bonds between people who experience it **together**. That's just what happened at Valley Forge!

A Prussian* nobleman volunteered to train George's troops in his beloved discipline.

*Prussia = another German state, like Hesse-Cassel*

GENERAL FRIEDRICH WILHELM LUDOLF GERHARD AUGUSTIN, BARON VON STEUBEN

Before the Revolution, people thought of themselves primarily as citizens of their individual colony first — Vermont or Maryland or North Carolina.

GONNA PUMP YOU UP!

But those soldiers from those different regions **drilled** together...

...and they replaced leaky tents with cabins they built **together**.

Though clothes were scarce, soldiers in a hut would gather up enough pieces between them to wrap up whoever was going out on guard duty.

For the first time, a **national** institution was being formed that brought **all** Americans together to think of themselves **as** Americans!

Valley Forge ended up being a happy time for George, too, because Martha came up from Mount Vernon to spend the winter with him.

Martha spent as much time with *George* in his camp as she could; in the end, George and Martha would be together for almost half the war, much to his delight.

Martha helped George by copying letters, visiting sick and wounded soldiers, and organizing social activities.

||||||()()|
(\||||||||||
[()|||||||||||)

Martha always brought a few slaves with her from Mount Vernon when she visited camp.

HEY...WAIT A MINUTE.

WHAT IF SLAVERY IS...

...WRONG?!

Spending so much time with people from different parts of the country started to change George's attitudes.

George had been born into a world where *slaveholding* was the norm. He had owned human beings since he was *eleven years old.*

But his three years fighting in the North had changed his mind about a lot of things.

He had already stopped allowing Mount Vernon's slave families to be broken up by sale – a frequent punishment for rebellious servants, as well as a common way for slave owners to raise money.

WHAT IF... WHAT IF I *SOLD OFF* ALL MY SLAVES? THEN I WOULD NO LONGER BE A SLAVE OWNER...

...BUT...*THAT* COULD BREAK UP FAMILIES... SEND THEM TO CRUELER MASTERS.... *I'D* BE RESPONSIBLE!

WHO WOULD WORK THE FARM? WHO WOULD TAKE CARE OF MARTHA? WHAT WOULD THE REST OF THE COUNTRY THINK?

The slavery question would trouble George for the rest of his life. He *did* change his mind about allowing more African Americans in the Continental Army, though.

The American cause was constantly struggling for new soldiers, and he saw how bravely black revolutionaries fought by his side.

His crossing of the Delaware was largely managed by John Glover's Marblehead regiment of different-race sailors!

Since the beginning of the war the **British** had offered *freedom* to any slaves who escaped to fight for the Crown.

Tens of thousands of African Americans fled their captors to sign up for black-only units like Virginia's "Ethiopian Regiment" and the elite "Black Brigade" – including *Henry Washington,* one of George's own Mount Vernon slaves.

Starting in 1778 George allowed colonies to raise different-race and black-only regiments of slaves with the same freedom-for-service deal.

African Americans fought *one another* on opposing sides of the Revolution.

**FOR FREEDOM!**

And white and black Americans would not fight side by side in the *same* units again until the *Korean War...170 years later!*

More help was on the way. After a major American victory, the French king, Louis XVI, agreed to join the war on the colonies' side. The American Revolution was now a *world war!*

YOU'RE JOINING US TO HELP THE FIGHT FOR LIFE, LIBERTY, AND THE PURSUIT OF HAPPINESS, RIGHT?

NO. *REVENGE!! REVENGE!!!*

EHH, CLOSE ENOUGH. WELCOME ABOARD!

(King of France from 1774 to Page 97)

The British Army was ordered to return to New York City from Philadelphia to protect against French invasion.

WE CAN'T STOP THEM, BUT WE CAN *ANNOY THE HECK* OUT OF THEM!

WE'RE *GOOD* AT THAT!

Though the British managed to get away, the battle proved, for the first time, that Colonial troops – helped by their European allies – could stand up to the trained forces of Great Britain.

BATTLE OF MONMOUTH
June 28, 1778: Continentals vs British + Hessians

THEY'VE BEEN *PRACTICING!* RUN!

The new British commander, *Henry Clinton*, had enough troops to guard New York but not enough to go after Washington.

GRRRRRR...

WHACK -A- COLONY

General Sir Henry Clinton (1730-1795), Fall Guy

George knew the army *was* the Revolution, and was smart enough never to march it into some place where it could be destroyed – he always kept it out of Clinton's reach.

Instead, Clinton decided to send a third of his army *south.* The South was believed to be more loyal to the Crown than the rest of the country, so they thought it would be easier to conquer.

After a couple more years of bloody *stalemate,* George and his French counterpart met in May 1781.

I HAVE RECEIVED WORD FROM PARIS THAT A MASSIVE FRENCH FLEET IS ON ITS WAY!

Joseph Webb House, Wethersfield, CT

Lt. Gen. Jean-Baptiste Donatien de Vimeur (1725–1807), Comte ("*Count*") de Rochambeau

THE TIME TO STRIKE A DECISIVE BLOW AGAINST CLINTON IS NOW!

WE SHOULD ATTACK *NEW YORK* AND DRIVE THE BRITISH OUT, ONCE AND FOR ALL!

I DON'T KNOW... THEY ARE *VERY* WELL POSITIONED THERE...

...AND BESIDES, OUR FRENCH SHIPS ARE MUCH *HEAVIER* THAN THE BRITISH! I FEAR THE WATERS OF NEW YORK HARBOR ARE TOO SHALLOW!

77

Meanwhile, in NYC...

THOSE *STUPID JERKS* ARE PLANNING TO ATTACK ME! I JUST *KNOW* IT!

Empire State Building
(won't be built for 150 years)

NYC

MY SOUTHERN COMMANDERS WANT ME TO SEND REINFORCEMENTS... BUT THAT COULD LEAVE *ME* OPEN TO ATTACK HERE!

WHAT TO DO?! IF ONLY THERE WAS SOME *SIGN*....

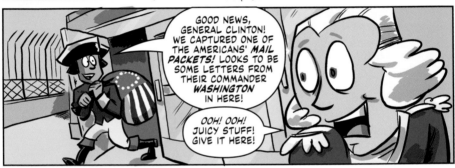

GOOD NEWS, GENERAL CLINTON! WE CAPTURED ONE OF THE AMERICANS' *MAIL PACKETS*! LOOKS TO BE SOME LETTERS FROM THEIR COMMANDER *WASHINGTON* IN HERE!

OOH! OOH! JUICY STUFF! GIVE IT HERE!

HAW! LOOK AT THIS ONE! IT'S TO HIS DENTIST IN PHILADELPHIA!

GENERAL GUMMY IS ASKING FOR... PINCERS? TO TIGHTEN THE WIRE...AROUND HIS *FALSE TEETH*?!

A-A-AND HE NEEDS A TOOTH SCRAPER! TO MAKE HIS *CHOMPERS* ALL WHITE AND *DAINTY*! HA-HA-HA!

OH, THAT'S BRILLIANT!

QUIET, YOU LOT! THERE ARE OTHER LETTERS IN HERE THAT SUGGEST AN ATTACK ON NEW YORK IS COMING SOON!

SEE THE FRENCH ARMY OVENS BAKING BREAD ALONG THE HUDSON?

SEE ALL THOSE BOATS THEY'RE READY TO LAUNCH?

ARE YOU SURE IT'S NOT A TRICK?

IMPOSSIBLE! WHAT MAN WOULD FAKE A LETTER ABOUT EMBARRASSING DENTAL PROBLEMS? THIS PACKET IS GENUINE!

WE WON'T REINFORCE THE SOUTH! WE'RE STAYING HERE!

HUZZAH!!!

Did George leak the packet on purpose so Clinton would stay put? Maybe.

# SIEGE of YORKTOWN

September 28 - October 19, 1781:
Continentals + French vs. British + Hessians

But the boats and ovens **were** distractions...

...Fooling Clinton into thinking New York was George's target, while he and Rochambeau marched their army south, into Virginia!

MY TEETH REALLY DO STILL *HURT*, THOUGH.... OW!

In the end, it was the admiral of the French Navy who decided to head to Chesapeake Bay in Virginia, to prevent the southern British army from escaping or being resupplied.

AAAH! IT'S THE FRENCH! RUN!

YOO-HOO!

NO! THEY'VE CUT US OFF BY LAND, TOO!

TRAPPED!! TRAPPED LIKE RATS!!

When the British surrendered, the war was basically over. America, with French help, had won independence –

— BUT NOW SHE HAD TO *KEEP* IT! THE STATES WEREN'T MAKING IT EASY *URK!* ACTING LIKE THIRTEEN SEPARATE COUNTRIES INSTEAD OF ONE "UNITED" NATION! *ACK!*

CONGRESS STILL COULDN'T RAISE NATIONAL TAXES *GASP!* AND SO THE CONTINENTAL ARMY WENT UNPAID!

Furious officers gathered in Newburgh, New York:

WE WILL MARCH ON PHILADELPHIA, OCCUPY CONGRESS, AND FORCE THOSE CROOKED POLITICIANS TO GIVE US OUR BACK PAY!

YEAH!

LET'S DO IT!

MAY *I* TALK TO THIS MEETING?

*GENERAL WASHINGTON!* UH — BUT OF COURSE, SIR....

LOOK. I KNOW IT'S FRUSTRATING YOU HAVEN'T BEEN PAID. BUT CONGRESS *IS* TRYING.

WE HAVE TO BE PATIENT, BUT TRUST THEY, IN THE END, WILL ACT *FAIRLY.*

THIS *REPUBLIC* WE ARE TRYING TO *MAKE* HERE HAS NEVER BEEN *TRIED* BEFORE.

SO PLEASE, *DON'T* START A *CIVIL WAR* SO SOON AFTER OUR REVOLUTION HAS BEEN WON, OR ALL OUR EFFORTS WILL END IN *FAILURE.*

WELL.

THAT'S ALL *I* CAME HERE TO SAY...

...BUT PLEASE, LET ME READ YOU A LETTER FROM A MEMBER OF CONGRESS WHO *SYMPATHIZES* WITH YOUR PROBLEMS....

REPRESENTATIVE JONES, FROM VIRGINIA, SAYS...

...HMM...

...THE HANDWRITING'S RATHER *SMALLER* THAN I THOUGHT....

GENTLEMEN, YOU WILL PERMIT ME TO PUT ON MY *SPECTACLES*...

"...FOR I HAVE NOT ONLY GROWN *GRAY* BUT ALMOST *BLIND* IN THE SERVICE OF MY COUNTRY."

By that simple act of humility, George had calmed the angry officers' hearts and stopped a revolution-*within*-the-revolution in its tracks.

They had that much love for this man, who had given up so much, that he was able to inspire them to continue to sacrifice.

Many in the army wanted George to seize power.

One literally wrote him and said he should become the *king of America*.

When he heard of it, no less an authority than *George III* of Great Britain said:

"IF HE DOES THAT, HE WILL BE THE *GREATEST MAN IN THE WORLD*."

SOMETIMES THE GREATNESS OF PEOPLE LIES IN WHAT THEY *DON'T* DO.

SO MANY REVOLUTIONS BEFORE AND SINCE BECAME BLOODY, VIOLENT TYRANNIES SO MUCH *WORSE* THAN THE ONES THEY OVERTHREW.

BUT NOT *AMERICA'S.*

BECAUSE ONE MAN, LEADING BY *EXAMPLE*, TURNED DOWN EVERY CROWN AND TITLE HE WAS OFFERED.

# THE AMERICAN

...is elected to four-year terms...

...by a super-duper-**complicated** system popularly known* as the ELECTORAL COLLEGE** appointed by each state.

PARRRR-TAAAAYYY!!

\* The term is not actually used in the Constitution

\*\* An old-timey meaning of the word: "an organization of professional people."

Only a **natural-born citizen** can be president, and you have to be 35 years old before you can run, and you need to have lived here at least 14 years.

I JUST **CRASHED** HERE **YESTERDAY** ON MY **FIFTH** BIRTHDAY!

THIS IS 100% **WRONG.**

You'll be elected with a **vice** president, who will take over for you if you die or quit or get fired ("**impeached**").

IT'S THE UNDERSTUDY'S TIME TO SHINE!

John Adams (1st Vice President//2nd President (\*\*SPOILERS\*\*))

# PRESIDENT...

You can't get a raise while in office!

AW C'MON, WHY NOOOOOOT?!?

You're the Commander in Chief of the *armed forces!*

YOU! GO FIGHT THOSE DUDES!

SIR, YES, SIR!

Only when you *sign* a bill does it become law (or it *doesn't* if you *veto* it)!

THIS REALLY, REALLY SOUNDS LIKE A *KING*, YOU GUYS!

BILL

You have to make treaties with other countries! Appoint judges! Ambassadors! And –

THIS SEEMS LIKE A BIG MISTAKE! WE'RE JUST GONNA GET RULED BY A *TYRANT* LIKE KING GEORGE AGAIN!

AW, C'MON, YOU DON'T HAVE TO WORRY ABOUT THE PRESIDENT *TURNING BAD!*

I MEAN, WE ALL *KNOW* WHO IT'S GONNA BE!

HOW COME?

WHO? *WHO?!?*

C'MON, GEORGE, YOUR COUNTRY NEEDS YOU!

*CAN'T MY COUNTRY NEED SOMEBODY ELSE FOR ONCE?!*

OH, RIGHT. DUH.

The Electoral College – in those days a very *exclusive* group of landowning white men – unanimously elected George the first president in 1789.

VOTE! VOTE! VOTE! VOTE! VOTE! VOTE! VOTE!

Not *everybody* was thrilled.

NO! GEORGE! DON'T GO! HEADING A GOVERNMENT IS TOO DANGEROUS! NOT MY GEORGIE-PORGIE!

MA. SERIOUSLY. I'M FIFTY-SEVEN YEARS OLD. THIS IS JUST SAD.

It took George and Martha eight days to travel from Mount Vernon to New York City, then the capital of the US.

Grand balls and parades were held in six states as people lined the streets to cheer on the new president.

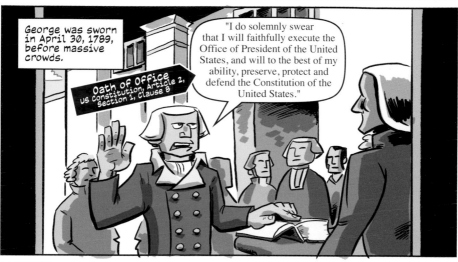

George was sworn in April 30, 1789, before massive crowds.

Oath of Office
US Constitution, Article 2, Section 1, Clause 8

"I do solemnly swear that I will faithfully execute the Office of President of the United States, and will to the best of my ability, preserve, protect and defend the Constitution of the United States."

As the first president, George established a lot of traditions every person who has held the office since still maintains...

Federal Hall, Wall Street, NYC

"THE PRESERVATION OF THE SACRED FIRE OF *LIBERTY*, AND THE DESTINY OF THE REPUBLICAN MODEL OF GOVERNMENT...

"...ARE JUSTLY CONSIDERED AS DEEPLY, PERHAPS AS FINALLY STAKED, ON THE *EXPERIMENT* ENTRUSTED TO THE HANDS OF THE AMERICAN PEOPLE."

...like giving an *inaugural address.*

The president doesn't have to run the Executive Branch by himself. The Constitution also suggests the president set up "executive departments," the secretaries of which form his main team of advisers.

The Secretary of War helps the Commander in Chief run the armed forces. George hired his artillery commander from the Battle of Trenton, *Henry Knox*, to do that.

The Attorney General, head of the Justice Department, helps the president with matters legal. George had his old lawyer from Virginia, *Edmund Randolph*, be the nation's *lawyer*.

The Secretary of State is the president's top diplomat. *Thomas Jefferson*, another Virginian and the author of the Declaration of Independence, had that job in the new government.

Last but not least *Alexander Hamilton*, one of Washington's most trusted aides during the war, headed up the Department of Treasury, which oversees government tax collection.

Today, we call this group the president's *"cabinet,"* after the *small room* where the King of England's Privy ("Private") Council met.

TOLD YOU! HE'S *SUCH A KING!*

DOWN IN FRONT!

The most immediate problem George and his cabinet had to solve was the crippling debt the US had built up during the revolution.

OOOH BOY.

SO, HERE'S MY PLAN: *WE*, THE FEDERAL GOVERNMENT, WILL *ASSUME* AND PAY ALL THE DEBTS OF THE *STATES*, TOO.

A *CENTRAL* BANKING SYSTEM WILL SIMPLIFY AND THEREFORE *STABILIZE* OUR ECONOMY!

*NO WAY, HAMILTON!* I SEE WHAT YOU'RE DOING: YOU'RE TRYING TO MAKE THE STATES *DEPENDENT* ON THE FEDS!

LOOK, JEFFERSON, WE CAN'T HAVE *THIRTEEN* DIFFERENT STATES WITH *THIRTEEN* DIFFERENT MONEY POLICIES!

YOUR WAY WILL LEAD TO *TYRANNY!*

*YOUR* WAY WILL LEAD TO *CHAOS!*

VIRGINIA HAS ALREADY *PAID OFF* ALL HER WAR DEBTS! WHY SHOULD *OUR* MONEY GO TO HELP PAY OFF THE IOUS OF *DEADBEAT* STATES?

VA

MA

MASSACHUSETTS IS UP TO OUR EYEBALLS IN DEBT! WE WILL *SECEDE* ("LEAVE THE UNION") IF YOU DON'T DO THIS PLAN!

WELL MAYBE *WE'LL* SECEDE IF THEY *DO!* NYAH!

(For more on how the states were always threatening to secede if they didn't get their way, see *Action Presidents: Abraham Lincoln!*)

HEY. HEY, HEY, HEY. HEY. ALEX.

BUDDY. *PAL.*

THIS CONSTANT *FIGHTING,* I THINK WE CAN BOTH AGREE, IT'S GETTING US *NOWHERE.*

YOU KNOW HOW WE'VE BEEN TALKING ABOUT BUILDING A PERMANENT *CAPITAL CITY,* AND EVERY STATE WANTS IT BUILT IN *THEIR* LAND?

UH-HUH?

ME! PICK ME!

SHUT UP, YOU! I'M THE BEST!

NO I AM!

WELL, WHAT IF — NOW I'M JUST *SPITBALLING* HERE — WHAT IF YOU GET ENOUGH *NORTHERN* VOTES TO GET THE CAPITAL PLACED IN THE *SOUTH?*

THEN I, AS A TOKEN OF, YOU KNOW, *FRIEND-SHIP*...I'LL GET MY SOUTHERN PALS BEHIND YOUR WACKY "DEBT ASSUMPTION" PLAN.

WHAT DO YOU SAY?

WELL... WE'LL HAVE TO CHECK WITH THE PRESIDENT *FIRST....*

HEY, GEORGE!

WHAT?

WHAT ARE YOUR THOUGHTS ON THE CAPITAL CITY'S LOCATION?

CAN IT BE NEAR MY HOUSE?

IN VIRGINIA? OF COURSE!

History would prove *Hamilton* right. Once he realized this, Jefferson called the deal he made for *Washington, DC* – a mere fifteen miles from its namesake's Mount Vernon – *the greatest mistake of his life.*

Now that Hamilton had all the *states'* debts too,
he had to figure out a way to pay them *off.*

BUT — I THOUGHT WE *FOUGHT* THE WAR BECAUSE OF *TAXES* IN THE FIRST PLACE!

AND YOU *WON* — CONGRATULATIONS!

TIME TO *PAY UP!*

So he had to take advantage of the Federal government's new power to tax.

First, Hamilton tried a tax on *whiskey* — the most popular form of booze in the country.

He thought that because it was a "sin tax" — making you *pay* more for something *bad* for you — people wouldn't object too much.

Unfortunately, whiskey was a vital product to western Pennsylvania farmers.

Their grain didn't stay fresh long enough to cross the Allegheny Mountains. However, distilling it into booze gave them a product to sell in eastern markets.

This started the *Whiskey Rebellion* in the west, where farmers attacked tax collectors and threatened to secede from the Union.

GIVE ME *LIQUOR* OR GIVE ME *DEATH!*

DON'T SPIT IN ME

96

On top of all *that*, like all the presidents *after* him, George also had to deal with problems coming in from the *rest* of the world too.

The US wasn't the only country to go broke during her Revolution. When *France* raised taxes during a famine to pay for her war debt, the people revolted!

ZUT ALORS! THEY NEVER TELL YOU HOW *EXPENSIVE* WARS ARE BEFORE YOU *START* THEM!

"Dang it!"

The *French* Revolution, which began in 1789, was far more brutal than America's. The king, queen, and other aristocrats got their heads cut off in the street!

CAN'T WE TALK ABOUT THIS?!?

Guillotine (gee-yo-teen): Proposed by Dr. Joseph Ignace Guillotin for really close shaves

THE FRENCH REVOLUTION IS *OBVIOUSLY* A CONTINUATION OF OUR OWN!

WE SHOULD *SUPPORT* THEM IN ANY WAY POSSIBLE!

ARE YOU NUTS, JEFFERSON? THE STREETS OF PARIS RUN WITH BLOOD!

THEY'RE NOTHING LIKE US! WE SHOULD STAY OUT OF IT!

YOU, HAMILTON, ARE A *MONOCRAT!*

A WHAT?

THAT'S A *NAME* I MADE UP FOR YOU THAT COMBINES THE WORD "MONARCHY" WITH THE WORD "DEMOCRAT."

IT MEANS YOU *SECRETLY* WANT A *KING!*

97

I DO *NOT*!

DO *TOO*!

SO DO *NOT* TIMES A *THOUSAND*!

SO DO *TOO* TIMES A THOUSAND AND *TWO*!

# ENOUGH!

WE'RE NOT GETTING INVOLVED! LET *EUROPE* DEAL WITH *EUROPE'S* PROBLEMS!

YOU *ALWAYS* TAKE HIS SIDE! *WHY?!*

NYAH!

THE USA WAS IN A *TOUGH SPOT* OVERSEAS. THOUGH SHE WAS A BIG COUNTRY IN TERMS OF SHEER SIZE, HER MILITARY WAS QUITE *WEAK*.

SHE COULDN'T AFFORD TO *ANGER* POWERFUL COUNTRIES LIKE GREAT BRITAIN, WHICH WENT TO WAR WITH FRANCE FOR TRYING TO EXPAND ITS "LETS KILL ALL THE KINGS" REVOLUTION BEYOND HER BORDERS!

SHE HAD NO ARMY OR NAVY TO SPEAK OF, LARGELY BECAUSE THE FRAMERS OF THE CONSTITUTION FEARED THE GOVERNMENT COULD TURN THAT MILITARY AGAINST THE PEOPLE.

Instead the Constitution suggests that the people themselves will be called upon to form militias, using their own weapons, when the need arises.

(But it's kind of hard to have a "militia navy.")

LET'S GET 'EM, BOYS! *YeeeHAH!!*

Still, in 1794 four states assembled a **"national militia"** of 12,950 men — more troops than George had at many times during the Revolution!

LISTEN UP, MEN! THESE "WHISKEY REBELS" ARE THREATENING TO SACK PITTSBURGH! THEY'RE BEATING UP TAX COLLECTORS AND ROBBING THE MAILS!

I'VE CALLED YOU HERE TO PUT A STOP TO IT!

FORTUNATELY, I KNOW THIS PART OF THE COUNTRY QUITE WELL!

OOOH! OOOH! BECAUSE THAT'S WHERE YOU AND BRADDOCK GOT YOUR BUTTS KICKED BY THE FRENCH, RIGHT, SIR?

YES, PRIVATE, THAT'S WHY.

I DIDN'T SEE SO MANY FRIENDS AND COMRADES *DIE* IN THE REVOLUTION JUST SO THE GOVERNMENT WE CREATED COULD GET *OVERTHROWN* BY ANYBODY WHO'S GOT A *BEEF* WITH IT!

BUT ISN'T THAT JUST WHAT YOU AND THE OTHER FOUNDING FATHERS DID WHEN YOU KICKED OUT KING GEORGE, SIR?

NO, NO. THAT WAS TOTALLY DIFFERENT.

BUT HOW?

*I'LL TELL YOU AFTER THE INVASION! ENOUGH WITH THE QUESTIONS!*

BUT FIRST, WE'RE GOING TO *MARCH* OVER THOSE MOUNTAINS, AND —

99

Had George led his force to Pittsburgh as planned, it would have been the *first* (and only!) time a sitting president actually *led* troops into battle.

MR. PRESIDENT... UH...*GENERAL? CHIEF? SIR!*

YOUR MILITIA *SCARED* THE REBELS, SIR. THEY'VE DISBANDED!

THE WHISKEY REBELLION IS OVER!

OH. WELL.

NEVER MIND, THEN.

WHO WANTS *BOILED TRIPE?*

BLAAAAGGH

FINE. MORE FOR ME, THEN.

George had desperately wanted to leave office back when his first term was up in 1793, but his advisers convinced him the government was still too weak to survive without him.

UGH...

GEORGE! GEORGE! GEORGE! GEORGE! GEORGE!

So, reluctantly, he let the Electoral College elect him unanimously to a *second* term, and what he called *"the extreme wretchedness of his existence"* continued....

100

OH... UH... OKAY...

I GUESS THAT'S A *NO*....

George announced his retirement in a "Farewell Address" he printed in the newspapers in 1796.

He pleaded with Americans to stay together and not break into political *parties.*

But as soon as he left office, the pro-Jefferson and pro-Hamilton sides of government did just *that.*

He told Americans to stay out of Europe's many wars.

But as soon as he left office, the *second* president, John Adams, founded the US Navy to fight France in a "Quasi-War."

quasi = "kinda looks like"

DOES THAT MEAN...I'M ONLY QUASI-*DYING?*

*KOF*!

NO, YOU'RE JUST *REGULAR-*DYING.

DANG... ACK!

WHY DID HE ALWAYS SUPPORT THAT HORRIBLE, GREEDY HAMILTON INSTEAD OF TOM JEFFERSON – A PLANTER, JUST LIKE US!

MAYBE HE ALWAYS *WAS* A BRITISH STOOGE....

Private citizen George Washington returned to Mount Vernon considerably *less* popular than President-Elect Washington was when he left eight years before.

Few were the people George told about his reasons for siding with Hamilton – and it wasn't just because they had served together in the war.

Hamilton's vision of America as an industrial powerhouse, centered in cities, would become true by the end of the next century.

But Jefferson's vision of America – based on huge plantations, supporting an elite planter class like in his Virginia – was possible only if one thing continued to survive – and thrive:

The free labor from *slavery.*

It's almost as if the outside threat of Britain kept Americans from fighting with each other over their differences.

In many parts of the country, antislavery forces moved quickly. Pennsylvania passed a law in 1780 that said slaves who lived in the state six months or longer were automatically *freed.*

This posed a problem for President Washington, who lived in Philadelphia, the second US capital, while Washington, DC, was being built.

To make sure none of the slaves who came from Mount Vernon to work in his house were freed, he'd send them away before six months was up, to "restart the clock."

One person who got herself off this merry-go-round was *Oney Judge*.

ELIZABETH, MY DEAREST GRANDDAUGHTER — WHEN I DIE, LOVELY ONEY, MY FAVORITE MAID, WILL BE YOURS!

*WHAT? NOBODY ASKED ME!*

Oney's free black friends in Philly helped smuggle her on a ship bound for New Hampshire one day when the Washingtons were out of town.

Martha was distraught. She thought maybe Oney had been fooled away by a boyfriend.

BUT SHE'S *MINE!* I WANT HER *BACK!*

THERE, THERE, MARTHA. LET ME SEE WHAT I CAN DO....

George sent his nephew after her, but the *governor of New Hampshire* himself warned Oney, and she went back into hiding.

I'LL ONLY COME BACK IF YOU PROMISE TO FREE ME WHEN YOU DIE!

YOU'RE MY *WIFE'S* SLAVE! I *CAN'T* PROMISE THAT!

THEN FORGET IT!

Thanks to the *Fugitive Slave Act* George himself signed into law, he could have kept pursuing Oney but didn't.

George was willing to free his slaves, but only on *his* terms.

He couldn't release them without losing a lot of money. A single field hand, man or woman, was worth as much as a small city lot, 3,000 pounds of beef, or 300 gallons of whiskey.

AM I SUPPOSED TO BE FLATTERED?

BECAUSE I'M NOT.

He tried to sell some land in the West he owned to finance emancipation, but couldn't find enough buyers.

He tried importing workers from England and Ireland to replace his slaves, but could not find any white people to do the backbreaking work African Americans performed daily!

He kept his attempts a secret, not wanting to get his slaves' hopes up – and to not earn the hatred of his slaveholding neighbors.

HEY! HE'S MAKIN' US LOOK BAD!

To a friend, George confided that if the North and the South went to war over slavery, he had *"made up his mind to move and be of the northern"* part of the country.

I GOT YOUR *BACK*, ABE!

WORD.

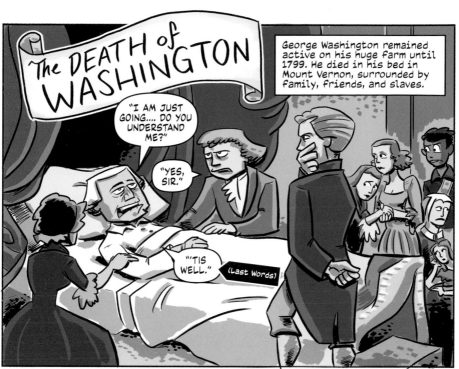

The DEATH of WASHINGTON

George Washington remained active on his huge farm until 1799. He died in his bed in Mount Vernon, surrounded by family, friends, and slaves.

"I AM JUST GOING.... DO YOU UNDERSTAND ME?"

"YES, SIR."

"'TIS WELL."

(Last Words)

His will contained some surprises – it freed his longtime personal servant William Lee outright, and freed all of George's own slaves upon Martha's death.

(Martha didn't wait that long, freeing *all* of George's slaves ten months after his death.)

This didn't apply to *Oney Judge*, who was one of *Martha's* slaves.

BUT THIS WAS *MY* IDEA IN THE *FIRST PLACE!!*

Fortunately, Martha's family left Oney alone. She married, had kids, and spent the rest of her life in New Hampshire.

HE WASN'T SOME *MYTHOLOGICAL DEMIGOD.* HE DID GOOD THINGS, AND HE DID BAD THINGS.

HE WAS A *PERSON,* LIKE YOU AND ME.

AND *THAT'S* WHAT MAKES ALL HE ACCOMPLISHED ALL THE MORE AMAZING!

*THAT'S* THE STATUE, OVER THERE!!

OOPS. SORRY.

SO, THE TRUTH IS ALWAYS *BETTER.* THAT'S WHAT YOU'RE SAYING?

YOU KNOW IT!

BUT...THAT'S EXACTLY WHAT THE *CHERRY TREE STORY* WAS SAYING, AND YOU SAID THAT WAS BAD.

UH...

AND THAT STORY WAS SUPER SHORT.

YEAH, WHAT YOU DID TOOK *WAY LONGER.*

UM...

NEWBURGH, NY:
CONTINENTAL ARMY
MUTINY

JOSEPH WEBB HOUSE,
WETHERSFIELD, CT

WASHINGTON'S
HEADQUARTERS, VALLEY
FORGE NATIONAL PARK,
PENNSYLVANIA

FEDERAL HALL, NYC
(1ST INAUGURATION)

INDEPENDENCE HALL,
PHILADELPHIA
(AND THE PRESIDENTIAL
HOUSE SITE NEARBY)

BOWLING GREEN, NYC
(WHERE KING GEORGE'S
STATUE WAS)

YORKTOWN
BATTLEFIELD PARK
(TECHNICALLY PART
OF COLONIAL
WILLIAMSBURG)

# TIMELINE

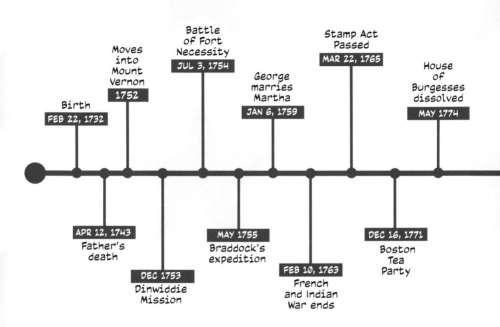

Birth
FEB 22, 1732

Moves into Mount Vernon
1752

Battle of Fort Necessity
JUL 3, 1754

George marries Martha
JAN 6, 1759

Stamp Act Passed
MAR 22, 1765

House of Burgesses dissolved
MAY 1774

APR 12, 1743
Father's death

DEC 1753
Dinwiddie Mission

MAY 1755
Braddock's expedition

FEB 10, 1763
French and Indian War ends

DEC 16, 1771
Boston Tea Party

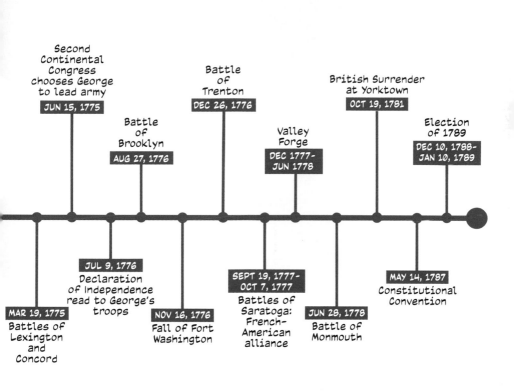

Second
Continental
Congress
chooses George
to lead army
JUN 15, 1775

Battle
of
Brooklyn
AUG 27, 1776

Battle
of
Trenton
DEC 26, 1776

Valley
Forge
DEC 1777-
JUN 1778

British Surrender
at Yorktown
OCT 19, 1781

Election
of 1789
DEC 10, 1788-
JAN 10, 1789

JUL 9, 1776
Declaration
of Independence
read to George's
troops

SEPT 19, 1777-
OCT 7, 1777
Battles of
Saratoga:
French-
American
alliance

MAY 14, 1787
Constitutional
Convention

MAR 19, 1775
Battles of
Lexington
and
Concord

NOV 16, 1776
Fall of Fort
Washington

JUN 28, 1778
Battle of
Monmouth

# GLOSSARY

**AMBUSH** (v): to attack unexpectedly from a hidden place

**ARTILLERY** (n): the troops charged with the use of mounted guns

**ASSUMPTION** (n): the act of taking ownership of something, specifically here of the colonies' debt (see below)

**BAYONET** (n): a small sharp sword attached to the end of a rifle's muzzle, used for hand-to-hand fighting

**CAMPAIGN** (n): a military operation with a specific goal or objective

**CANISTER** (n): a can filled with a whole bunch of little cannonballs that can be shot from a cannon in lieu of cannonballs

**DEBT** (n): something that is owed to another person or entity

**EMANCIPATION** (n): the act of freeing someone from slavery

**HIGHLAND** (n): a mountainous region

**INAUGURATION** (n): the act of installing a person in a position of power, usually during a formal ceremony

**LEGISLATURE** (n): a body of people who are charged with drafting and changing the laws of a country and/or state

**LOOT** (v): to steal, especially in times of war

**MILITIA** (n): a group of citizen soldiers, usually not employed full-time in military service and often not professionally trained

**MUZZLE** (n): the end of the barrel of a gun

**REINFORCEMENTS** (n): an additional supply of personnel for military service

**REPUBLIC** (n): a country in which the leader is not a king or queen

**SECEDE** (v): to withdraw from membership in a group or union

**SLOOP** (n): a sailing vessel with a single mast

**TYRANNY** (n): an unjust government ruled by a tyrant or dictator

**WITHDRAWAL** (n): in war, the act of retreating

# STUFF NAMED AFTER WASHINGTON

**NINE COLLEGES**

**SEVEN MOUNTAINS**

**TEN LAKES**

**EIGHT STREAMS**

**THE FIRST BALLISTIC SUBMARINE**

# BIBLIOGRAPHY

Cook, Don. *The Long Fuse: How England Lost the American Colonies, 1760-1785.* New York: Atlantic Monthly Press, 1996. There's two sides to every story, and this is a very good look at how Great Britain saw the American Revolution.

Ellis, Joseph J. *Founding Brothers: The Revolutionary Generation.* New York: Vintage Books, 2002. The classic look at how the Founding Fathers influenced one another; an excellent source to understand the two terms of the Washington presidency.

Finegan, Sr., Jeffrey E. *Colonel Washington and Me.* Siegle Books, 2012. A picture book about the life of George's slave valet, William Lee.

Fischer, David Hackett. *Washington's Crossing.* New York: Oxford University Press, 2004. The best book about the Battle of Trenton, it looks at the American, British, and Hessian sides – and reads like a movie thriller!

Flexner, James Thomas. *Washington: The Indispensable Man.* New York: Back Bay Books, 1994. The lavishly illustrated version of a classic biography of our George.

Kennedy, Frances H., ed. *The American Revolution: A Historical Guidebook.* New York: Oxford University Press, 2014. A great guide to places (that you can visit!) and battles (with maps!) with views from many different historians. Proceeds from the book go to the Conservation Fund's efforts to preserve historic places.

Morison, Samuel Eliot, ed. *Sources & Documents Illustrating the American Revolution 1764–1788 and the Formation of the Federal Constitution,* 2nd ed. New York: Oxford University Press, 1965. All the famous documents of the time period, plus selections from the debates that shaped them.

Nagy, John A. *Invisible Ink: Spycraft of the American Revolution,* 2nd ed. Yardley, PA: Westholme Publishing, 2011. If codes, ciphers, and devious doings are your thing, then this is the book about America's beginning for you!

Washington, George. *George Washington's Rules of Civility & Decent Behaviour in Company and Conversation.* Carlisle, MA: Applewood Books, 1988. Well, George didn't write this, he copied it from a French book on etiquette, but it's still an interesting historical curiosity.